THE CHILDREN OF SANDY HOOK
VS.
THE U.S. CONGRESS AND GUN
VIOLENCE IN AMERICA

THE CHILDREN OF SANDY HOOK

VS.

THE U.S. CONGRESS AND GUN VIOLENCE IN AMERICA

DENNY TAYLOR

GARN PRESS
NEW YORK, NY

Published by Garn Press, LLC
New York, NY
www.garnpress.com

Book and cover design by Benjamin J. Taylor/Garn Press

First Edition, March 2017

Library of Congress Control Number: 2017939400

Publisher's Cataloging-in-Publication Data

Names: Taylor, Denny
Title: The children of Sandy Hook vs. the U.S. Congress and gun
    violence in America / Denny Taylor.
Description: New York : Garn Press, 2017.
Identifiers: LCCN 2017939400 | ISBN 978-1-942146-59-9 (pbk.) |
    ISBN 978-1-942146-60-5 (Kindle ebook)
Subjects: LCSH: Children and violence. | Firearms--Law and
    legislation. | Assault weapons--Law and legislation. | Gun
    control. | BISAC: SOCIAL SCIENCE / Violence in Society. |
    POLITICAL SCIENCE / Political Process / Political Advocacy.
    | POLITICAL SCIENCE / Corruption & Misconduct. |
    POLITICAL SCIENCE / Public Policy / Social Policy. |
    POLITICAL SCIENCE / Propaganda.
Classification: LCC HQ784.V55.T39 2017 (print) | DDC 324.0207--
    dc23.
Library of Congress record available at https://lccn.loc.
    gov/2017939400

In Memoriam

*In memory of the 20 kindergarten
children and 6 educators who lost their
lives in the Newtown Massacre*

Dedication

*To the families and friends of those who
have lost their lives in U.S. massacres,
and to all those who are courageous
when mass killings occur*

In Condemnation

*In condemnation of the Members of
Congress who voted against the 2013
Assault Weapons Ban bill, for their
willingness to sacrifice the lives of
America's children to protect the assault
weapons that killed them*

Contents

INTRODUCTION

During the 2016 election President Donald Trump entered into a pact with the NRA "To make America free again". Adam Winkler, a law professor at the University of California-Los Angeles states, "They are tight with Trump Administration. They have their people in place and they know exactly what they're going for." Already Senator John Cornyn (R-TX), who was instrumental in defeating the 2013 Assault Weapons Ban bill, has had a bill read twice and referred to the Senate Judiciary Committee.

The situation is grave and urgently needs to be understood. This book, *The Children Of Sandy Hook vs. The US Congress And Gun Violence In America* is a provocative analysis of the vast gap between the American people who are intent on protecting children and the people who are intent on protecting guns whatever the cost to U.S. society. The book is about the ethical failure of the pro-gun Senators who deceived the American people with the arguments they presented that led to the failure of the Assault Weapons Ban bill in 2013. Documentation is presented to support the contention that when the Senators' *theoretical* arguments are juxtaposed with the *real life accounts* of the Sandy Hook Massacre, their deceptive language strategies for defeating the Assault Weapons Ban bill are exposed.

If we as a people are to regain our humanity the madness must stop. The members of the U.S. Congress who voted against the 2013 Assault Weapons Ban bill and the bills of 2016 must look at themselves and change their behavior. They can no longer represent the gun lobby that is selling the military style guns, which are being used in mass killings of American people. They need to know that democracy breaks down when those who govern condone violence against the nation's own children. From the very young to the very old, people of every race and ethnic group, across class, gender, and sexual orientation, the U.S. Congress is putting the entire population at risk. The Senators and Members of the House of Representatives who voted against the 2013 and 2016 Assault Weapons bills can no longer be blinded to the consequences of their actions. They must listen to the American people and the organizations that represent them.

GUN VIOLENCE IN AMERICA

More than 1000 mass killings have taken place in the United States since 20 little children and 6 educators were gunned down in Sandy Hook Elementary School on December 14, 2012. Since that heinous crime it is estimated that guns have been used to kill more than 90,000 Americans and injure more than 210,000 people. Included in these statistics are the deaths of more than 500 children.

United in grief, this violence against a country of peaceful people cannot be allowed to triumph. If we value democracy, if we value human rights, we cannot allow the mass killing of peaceful people to continue. We need our children, our loved ones, *and* U.S. society to be secure.

What connects the deaths of the 49 people killed and 53 injured in the Pulse Nightclub in Orlando, Florida with the deaths of 20 six and seven year old children and 6 adults at the Sandy Hook Elementary School, Newtown, Massachusetts, is the gun of choice used by Omar Marteen in Orlando and Adam Lanza in Newtown. Both shooters used a military style AR-15 rifle in their heinous massacres -- Marteen a Sig Sauer Model MCX, and Lanza a Bushmaster model XM15 rifle.

After the massacre, search warrants show that Adam Lanza still had three unused magazines for the Bushmaster, each of them containing 30 rounds, and ammunition for a Glock 10mm handgun and a 9mm Sig Sauer P226 handgun, which he'd taken with him to the elementary school. In the area of the shootings were six additional 30-round magazines which contained 0, 0, 0, 10, 11 and 13 live rounds, respectively. In total, 154 spent .223 casings were recovered from the scene, and investigators believe that the shooting only lasted five minutes. Every 15 seconds a little child was killed -- some quite literally blown away.

The massacre of 20 innocent little children and six educators at the Sandy Hook Elementary

School was supposed to have been a defining moment in the United States. It was supposed to be the last time a battle proven weapon system was used to kill American children and adults in such a heinous act. It was not.

"Shooter make ready," gun manufacturers command in adverts for the AR-15, which is promoted on the Web as a "complete weapon system for any scenario or environment" and as "an innovated weapon system build around a battle proven core."

The NRA calls the AR-15 the gun of choice for "home defense". There are approximately 3,700,000 AR-15's in the hands of civilians in the U.S, including Senators and Member of the House of Representatives -- some of whom boasted of their assault weapon ownership following the Sandy Hook Massacre during the Senate Hearings on the failed 2013 Assault Weapons Ban bill.

Would the Charleston, San Bernardino, Orlando and Dallas Massacres have taken place if the Assault Weapons Ban bill had passed? Unlikely. Research on gun violence conducted more than 20 years ago by the Center for Disease Control (CDC) -- *before* the NRA pressured the US Congress to withdraw all CDC funding on gun violence research -- provides sufficient evidence for the conclusion to be reached that people in America would be safer and the people who died in Charleston, San Bernardino, Orlando and Dallas would have been alive today if military style assault weapons had been banned in the U.S. in 2013.

THE BILL TO BAN ASSAULT WEAPONS IN THE AFTERMATH OF THE SANDY HOOK MASSACRE

In the aftermath of the Sandy Hook the outpouring of grief from the American people was immense, and so was the global outrage and condemnation of America for the barbaric protection of automatic weapons by Congress that endanger the lives of children and adults in U.S. society. The sale of assault weapons had to be stopped.

But before there are mass killings, Assault Weapons Ban bills must be killed by the U.S. Congress. Wars of words take place, with some Senators bragging about the assault weapons they own, while other Senators enter the arena without any weaponry and express their fear of the

Gun Lobby's arsenal.

On February 27, 2013 Senator Dianne Feinstein held a news conference to announce she was putting forth a bill to ban the sale of assault weapons. At the news conference Dianne Feinstein read the statement quoted here, which describes the bill and frames subsequent Senate Hearings:

> We are holding today's hearing because the massacre in Newtown was, sadly, not an anomaly. From the 1966 shooting rampage at the University of Texas, to the Newtown massacre, we have witnessed an increasing number of these mass killings..

> Since 1982, there have been at least 62 mass shootings across the United States. And they have been accelerating in recent years: 25 of these shootings have occurred since 2006, and seven took place in 2012.

> The one common thread running through these mass shootings in recent years— from Aurora, Colorado, to Tucson, Arizona, to Blacksburg, Virginia —

is that the gunman used a military-style, semiautomatic assault weapon or large-capacity ammunition magazine to commit the unspeakable horror ...

We cannot allow the carnage I have described to continue without taking action. That is why I joined with many of my colleagues on this Committee – **Senators Schumer, Durbin, Whitehouse, Klobuchar, Franken, Blumenthal and Hirono**, as well as many others off the committee -- to introduce legislation to prohibit the sale, transfer, manufacture, and importation of assault weapons and high-capacity magazines.

Senator Feinstein stated, "You can buy what's called a "bump fire stock" legally that you insert into an AR-15 or other assault rifles." She noted, "this device is legal, and it allows a semiautomatic firearm to be fired as quickly as a fully automatic machinegun, which has been banned for decades." She then described the key features of the proposed new "Assault Weapons Ban of 2013" bill:

- The bill bans the sale, transfer, importation, and manufacturing of 157 specifically named semiautomatic assault weapons.

- It also bans any other assault weapon, which is defined as a semiautomatic weapon that can accept a detachable magazine and has one military characteristic, such as a pistol grip, barrel shroud, or folding stock. These features were developed for military weapons to make them more effective and efficient at killing people in close-combat situations.

- The bill prohibits large-capacity ammunition feeding devices capable of accepting more than 10 rounds. This is a crucial part of this legislation. These large magazines and drums make a gun especially dangerous, because they allow a shooter to fire 15, 30, even 100 rounds or more without having to pause to reload. In many instances, like the tragic shooting of our colleague Congresswoman Gabby Giffords in Tucson, Arizona, it is only when the shooter has to stop to change magazines that police or others have the chance to take the shooter down.

Dianne Feinstein also stated that the bill protects the rights of legitimate gun owners:

- First, it will not affect hunting or sporting firearms. Instead, the bill protects legitimate hunters by specifically excluding over 2,000 specifically named firearms used for hunting or sporting purposes.

- Second, the bill will not take away any weapons that anybody owns today. Anyone who says otherwise is simply trying to deceive you. Instead, the bill grandfathers weapons legally possessed on the date of enactment.

- Finally, while the bill permits the continued possession of high-capacity ammunition magazines that are legally possessed on the date of enactment, it would ban the future sale or transfer of these magazines.

She also addressed the charge that assault weapons bans such as those in the proposed bill are unconstitutional:

The original federal assault weapons ban was challenged repeatedly in federal court, on every ground that opponents could come up with, including the Second Amendment, the Ninth Amendment, the Commerce Clause, the Due Process clause, equal protection and being a bill of attainder. Each and every time these challenges were rejected and the ban was upheld, including by the Fourth, Sixth, Ninth, and D.C. Circuits.

As we all know, the Supreme Court subsequently recognized the individual right to gun ownership in *District of Columbia v. Heller.* However, that decision clearly stated AND I QUOTE, that "the right secured by the Second Amendment is not unlimited." 554 U.S. 570, 626 (2008). Justice Scalia, the author of that opinion, wrote that "dangerous and unusual weapons" could be prohibited. *Id.* at 627.

Following *Heller*, state assault weapons bans in California and the District of Columbia have been upheld as consistent with the Second Amendment, in *People v. James*, 174 Cal.App.4th 662 (2009), and *Heller v. District of Columbia,* 670 F.3d

1244 (2011) (known as "*Heller II*").

In her speech at the press conference Dianne Feinstein spoke of the support for the bill to ban assault weapons by U.S. law enforcement, health care professionals, education and child welfare organizations, gun safety groups, religious groups of all faiths and denominations and other organizations. The weight of the people, across all walks of life, in every profession, and of every political persuasion, is represented. However, the National Rifle Association is noticeably *missing* from the list, which is included at the end of this post.

The almost universal endorsement of the 2013 Assault Weapons Ban bill leave us in no doubt of the high degree of consensus in U.S. society for the elimination of assault weapons – a consensus as great or greater than on any other issue confronting the American people. But moral outrage in the U.S. is tempered by fear -- fear of the NRA -- not only by a peaceful public, but also the fear of Members of Congress who supported the Assault Weapons Ban bill struggle to find the courage to confront the enormous power of the multi-billion-dollar gun industry.

SENATE COMMITTEE HEARING ON THE BILL TO BAN ASSAULT WEAPONS, FEBRUARY 27, 2013

At the February 27th Senate Committee Hearing on the 2013 Assault Weapons Ban bill the arguments presented by pro-gun Senators for the protection of the Bushmaster that Lanza used to kill the kindergarten children, stand in stark contrast to the expressions of grief of the father of a slain child and the testimony of the trauma surgeon who was in the ER when the bodies of the children arrived at the hospital.

The Congressional Hearing was filled with extremely polite political hostilities, even hatreds. Hypotheticals were used to challenge events, and unsupported opinions presented to contest the evidence. Questions and commentary by pro-gun

Senators, seemingly considered in the moment, were actually carefully rehearsed.

There were patterns in the discourse – tricks of the trade. Attend briefly. Avoid attending during descriptions of killings.Come and go. Acknowledge that a terrible event had taken place and move on. Do not engage. Shift the narrative from graphic details of twenty kids dying to a woman in a closet when an intruder enters her house. Literally. Use the woman to kill the conversation about the dead children whose bodies had been obliterated. Reposition the AR-15 assault rifle from deadly weapon to lifesaver – even though it is not1. Give the woman a child. Twist emotions. Call the assault weapon "women's gun of choice". Appear to be caring. Neutralize the reaction – feminize the gun. It's a gun with accessories, a lady's gun. Then move on. Focus on the Constitution. Lecture. Pontificate. *Drone on.*

Neil Heslin whose son Jesse, was killed by Adam Lanza at the Sandy Hook Elementary

---

1   Miller, Matthew; Azrael, Deborah; Hemenway, David. Firearm availability and unintentional firearm deaths, suicide, and homicide among women. Journal of Urban Health. 2002; 79:26-38.

School Massacre testified at the Senate Gun Hearing. When Neil Heslin began his testimony, he was holding a large framed photograph of Jesse when he was three months old in his Dad's arms. (This account includes his oral commentary combined with his written testimony.)

"On December 14, Jesse got up and got ready for school," Neil Heslin said. "He was always excited to go to school. I remember on that day we stopped by Misty Vale Deli. It's funny the things you remember. I remember Jesse got the sausage, egg and cheese he always gets, with some hot chocolate. And I remember the hug he gave me when I dropped him off. He just held me, and he rubbed my back. I can still feel that hug."

"And Jesse said, 'It's going to be alright. Everything's going to be okay, Dad.' Looking back it makes me wonder. What did he know? Did he have some idea about what was about to happen? But at the time I didn't think much of it. I just thought he was being sweet."

"Jesse just had this idea that you never leave people hurt. If you can help somebody, you do it. If you can make somebody feel better, you do it. If you can leave somebody a little better off, you do it."

"They tell me that's how he died. I guess we still don't know exactly what happened at that school. Maybe we'll never know. But what people tell me is that Jesse did something different. When he heard the shooting, he didn't run and hide. He started yelling. People disagree on the last thing he said. One person who was there says he yelled, 'run!' Another person said he told everybody to 'run now.' Ten kids from my son's class made it to safety. I hope to God something Jesse did helped them survive that day."

"What I know is that Jesse wasn't shot in the back. He took two bullets. The first one grazed the side of his head, but that didn't stop him from yelling. The other hit him in the forehead. Both bullets were fired from the front. That means the last thing my son did was look Adam Lanza straight in the face and scream to his classmates to run."

Neil Heslin was sobbing.

"I wish I wasn't here with you today. The best day of my life was the day my son was born. The worst day was the day he died. I don't want to relive that day talking to you here about it. It would be easier for me just to stay home."

"But I know that's not what Jesse would do. Jesse died screaming at a man with a gun. He died yelling at the top of his lungs so maybe some of his classmates could get to safety. I'm not going to scream at you, but I hope that maybe I can use my voice like my son used his. Maybe if I make enough noise a few beautiful innocent children like my Jesse won't have to die."

"I'm not real political. Half the time I think it doesn't matter which group of you guys runs things out here, no offense. I've always thought it wasn't a real good idea for people to be walking around the streets with military weapons, but I probably wouldn't have said anything about it."

"But right now this isn't about politics. So the reason I say this isn't about politics is because what I felt on that day, and what I've felt since, doesn't have anything to do with politics."

"In politics, people like to debate and say if we banned the weapon Adam Lanza used would he have just found something else. But let me tell you, when you're sitting at a firehouse and it's one in the morning and you're hoping against hope that your son is still hiding somewhere in that school, you want any change that makes it one bit more likely you'll see your boy again. If keeping those unnecessary weapons off the street would have let one more of those children leave that school building, it might have been my Jesse. If Adam Lanza had been able to shoot just one fewer bullet, maybe my son would be with me today."

"Jesse was the love of my life," Neil Heslin said, his voice filled with emotion. "He was the only family I had left. It's hard for me to be here today to talk about my deceased son. I have to. I'm his voice. It was 9:04 when I dropped Jesse off. Jesse gave me a hug and a kiss and at that time said goodbye and love you. He stopped and said, 'I love mom too.'"

"That was the last I saw of Jesse as he ducked around the corner," in gut wrenching grief he continued. "When he was getting out of the truck he hugged me and held me and I can still feel that hug and pat on the back and he said, 'Everything's going to be okay Dad. It's all going to be okay.'"

"It wasn't okay," Neil Heslin sobbed, crying

openly in front of the Senators. "I have to go home at night to an empty house without my son."

Following Neil Heslin, William Begg testified. Dr. Begg was one of the physicians in the emergency room the day of the Newtown shooting, and again this account includes his oral commentary combined with his written testimony.

"I am a parent of students in the Newtown School District," William Begg explained. "I have practiced emergency medicine at the Danbury Hospital Emergency Room in Connecticut and helped found and develop our region's trauma center."

"Let me begin by saying that my heart goes out to the 26 families from Sandy Hook Elementary that lost their spouses, their parents, and their children in the worst mass murder of children the US has seen in the last century. Newtown is still hurting badly. Many first responders have not returned to work and many of our children have not returned to school."

"Yet, what forever changed my life was being the Emergency Room physician that was on shift at Danbury Hospital on December 14th - the day of the horrific shooting at Sandy Hook Elementary School. This event has forever changed our community and my life."

"I have seen many gun related deaths over the past 25 years. I witnessed an assault weapons related death my first day in a hospital as medical student in New York City in 1987. My experiences in Baltimore and NYC with assault rifle deaths are vivid memories I will never forget."

"Since many people outside of law enforcement, the military or the emergency room have never seen the destruction that a gunshot can cause on the human body, I have included several pictures. Note that these pictures are not from the Sandy Hook Massacre, as it would be highly inappropriate to show such pictures in deference to the Sandy Hook families and in respect of HIPAA laws."

The photos William Begg presented to the Senators with his testimony were graphic, leaving them in no doubt about the wounds of the little children shot to death by Adam Lanza.

"Each of the children murdered at Sandy Hook Elementary had reportedly three to eleven bullet wounds per the report of Dr. Wayne Carver, the Connecticut State Chief Medical Examiner on December 15, 2012," William Begg stated. He stressed, "These pictures should in no way be construed as representing any of the actual injuries sustained by any of the victims from the Sandy Hook Massacre on December 14, 2012."

"Unfortunately, mass shootings have happened all around the world," Begg stated. "For example, in 1996, in Dunblane, Scotland, a 43-year-old gunman entered an elementary school and fired his weapons 109 times shooting 27 children and 4 teachers; killing 16 children and one teacher. He then shot and killed himself." Begg gives another example. 1996. Port Arthur, Australia. A 28-year-old with an AR-15 rifle and shot 35 people dead and wounded another 23 people.

"The difference with these cases and the tragic string of mass shootings at Columbine, Virginia Tech, Aurora, Oak Creek and so many others," Begg told the committee, "is that legislators in those countries acted by passing reasonable gun violence measures. In response to the incident in Scotland, meaningful gun legislation was enacted, that still permitted certain sporting guns, historic handguns, and selected other guns. Gun laws in Australia, which had been relatively lenient before the Port Arthur Massacre, were reviewed and tightened significantly after the incident. Australians who want to purchase a gun now must have an extensive background check. Semi-automatic gun and assault type rifles were banned."

"Did the legislation make a difference right away?" William Begg asked. "Actually, in some instances, it didn't. After many years though, the effects of real gun legislation did decrease gun related deaths." He cited the data. "According to a December 17, 2012 article in Time World, the results of the Australian law were significant. A widely cited 2010 study in the American *Journal of Law & Economics* showed that gun-related homicides in Australia dropped 59% between 1995 and 2006. The firearm-suicide rate dropped 65%."

"While the generation preceding the Port Arthur tragedy there had been over a dozen mass shootings, there have been no mass shooting in Australia since 1996," William Begg stated. "Furthermore, despite a surge in gun-related offenses in the early 2000s, the past seven years in the U.K. have seen successive drops in gun crimes."

Later in his testimony Begg urged Congress to "End the freeze on gun related research, as the CDC and other scientific agencies have been barred by Congress from using funds to "advocate or promote gun control".

"Assault rifle gun deaths include many that tragically don't even make it to the ER because the bodies are so badly mutilated they are pronounced dead in the field," William Begg stated. "Comprehensive research would allow governing bodies to collate data from a multitude of agencies.

"Conduct research on the causes and prevention of gun violence; including links between video games, media images, and violence. Please let us do gun research that is real."

"Protect the rights of health care providers to talk to their patients about gun safety," Begg pleaded that the Federal legislature "Clarify that no federal law prevents health care providers from warning law enforcement authorities about threats of violence."

"We are being intimidated not to discuss gun violence as a public health issue," he stated. "I accept one's Second Amendment right to own a gun if one goes through the proper channels. On the other hand, when I educate my patients on the effects of unsafe sex, morbid obesity, tobacco use, excessive alcohol use, texting and driving, or seatbelt use, please allow me as a medical doctor to talk to them about the risks of gun ownership - *please*?"

In his written testimony entered into the Congressional Record William Begg included the scientific research on the risks of gun ownership, leaving no doubt that if you buy a gun with the idea of protecting yourself and your family, the data is quite clear that you have an *increased* chance of dying from gun related injuries. The research demonstrates that:

- Homicide risk significantly increases if there is a gun in the home.

- Women are five times as likely to die of gun violence from their partner if there is a gun in the home.

- Two-thirds of women killed by spouses are killed with guns.

- A gun stored in the home is associated with a threefold increase in the risk of homicide.

- Suicide risk significantly increases if there is a gun in the home.

- A gun stored in the home is associated with a fivefold increase in the risk of suicide.

- Victims of suicide living in homes with guns were more than 30 times more likely to have died from a firearm-related suicide than from one committed with a different method.

- Owning any gun significantly increases your risk of being shot.

- People possessing a gun were more than 4 times more likely to be shot in an assault than those not possessing a gun.

- Unintentional gun death significantly increased if you own a gun.

- You are 28 times more likely to die of an unintentional gun death if you own a gun.

- You have a significantly increased chance

that you or your spouse or your kids are going to be killed from your own gun related to domestic homicide, suicide or accidental death.

William Begg stressed that this data must be available to those who are considering buying a gun out of fear of being killed from a potential intruder. Based on his first hand account of the Sandy Hook Massacre and his presentation of the scientific evidence he urged the U.S. Congress to ban military-style assault weapons.

"As a result of this growing gun violence epidemic," William Begg told the Senators, "more than half of the largest mass murders in our country's history have taken place since Columbine. Mass shootings are a slowly growing cancer in our society that must be addressed now."

"Folks say, in the big scheme of things there are not that many assault weapons deaths in our country," William Begg continued, the emotion in his voice was clearly audible. "*Please* don't tell that to the people from Columbine, from Virginia Tech, from Tucson, from Aurora, from Wisconsin. And definitely do not tell that to the families of

Newtown."

The people from Newtown at the hearing clapped as William Begg struggled to continue. "Don't tell that to the people in Newtown," he said openly crying. "This is a *tipping point*. This is a tipping point and this is a *public health issue*. *Please* make the right decision."

The gut wrenching descriptions by Neil Heslin and William Begg of the Sandy Hook Massacre were defining moments in the argumentation for the 2013 Assault Weapons Ban bill. There was an expectation that Neil Heslin's account of the extraordinary bravery of an American six-year-old boy – his son Jesse -- who shouted to his school friends to run and who was facing his killer when he was shot in the head, would be met with moral outrage by the pro-gun U.S. Senators. But it was not. Similarly, there was an expectation that William Begg's graphic description of what happens to a young child's body when it was hit by eleven bullets from an automatic weapon would sway the pro-gun Senators. Once again, it was not. Instead, brutality triumphed over tragedy, leaving no doubt that in the U.S. automatic weapons are protected but little children are not.

"Thank you for inviting me," the next person to testify said, before he twisted the rhetoric in his pro-assault weapon lamentation. "First I should say sitting through the last two pieces of testimony I'll just affirm the instinct that when one listens to events like this the impulse is to give them anything they want. And I would say to people who support the bill that I have a critique here and that mine is a counsel of despair."

And with that, this pro assault weapon testifier stole the moments when a father and a surgeon cried during their testimony about the last moments of a son's life and the terrible deaths of twenty very young children. In this way genuine grief was turned into a rhetorical device to support the pro-gun Senators rejection of the Assault Weapon's Ban bill.

At the highest level of government the twisted patterns of discourse -- the *tyranny of language* -- left no doubt that the mission of the pro-assault weapon Senators was to protect the gun by steering the hearings and sub-committee meetings away from the Sandy Hook Massacre. There was too much at stake. The cost-benefit ratio was too high. In other words the loss of revenues and profits *cost* of banning the AR-15 and similar weapons was too *high* to remotely consider such a humane act as saving the lives of American citizens or their children.

At the end of the Hearing only Senators Feinstein, Blumenthal, and Franklin were still present. The pro-gun Senators had left.

EXPRESSIONS OF PUBLIC GRIEF IN THE AFTERMATH OF THE MASS KILLING OF FIVE AND SIX YEAR OLD CHILDREN

On December 19, 2012, five days after the Sandy Hook Massacre I drove with a doctoral student to Newtown, Connecticut. Every car park was full and ribbons of cars were parked for miles alongside every country road and people were walking quietly carrying teddy bears and flowers, past historic old New England homes that had been decorated for the holidays, that now had decorated signs of condolence in windows and on their front doors. On one front lawn angels to celebrate the Christmas birth were dedicated to the dead little children.

Quietly and unobtrusively we photographed

the prayers, poems, cards of condolence, draw-
ings, and notes – *any* text which contained words,
symbols, or pictorial images – and then moved on
to photograph the flowers, balloons, teddy bears
and toys people had left in memoriam of the 20
kindergarten children and six educators.

Our task was to make sure that for a few hours
on this one day, every message was carefully photographed and preserved, before the thousands of
flowers, candles, letters, prayers, signs, photos,
toys and teddy bears were gathered and pro-
cessed into sacred soil for permanent memorial in
Newtown.

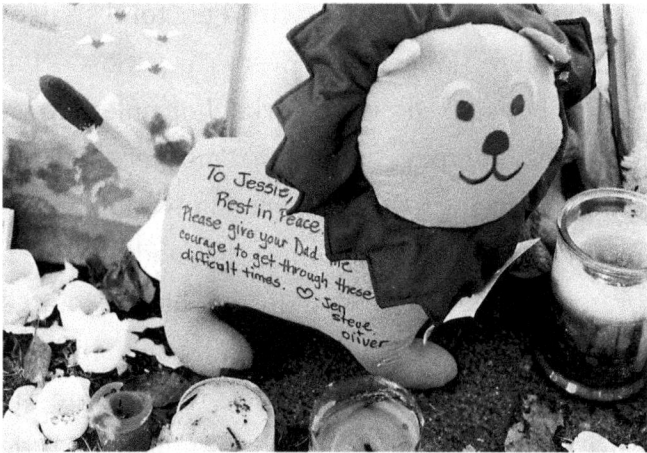

One message in black marker on the side of
an orange lion with a brown mane was written

to Neil Heslin's son, Jesse: *"To Jessie, Rest in Peace. Please give your Dad the courage to get through these difficult times. Jen, Steve, and Oliver."*

A small white cross with 12-14-12 with Ann Marie Murphy printed on it was nestled between other beautiful objects that had been left, and inside a glass ball was written: *"My dearest angel, may you enter the gates of heaven with your wings held high and a smile upon your face. Tell god your story so that he will remember always. He will love you as we do below. Even though you are gone now, you will forever be held in our hearts.*

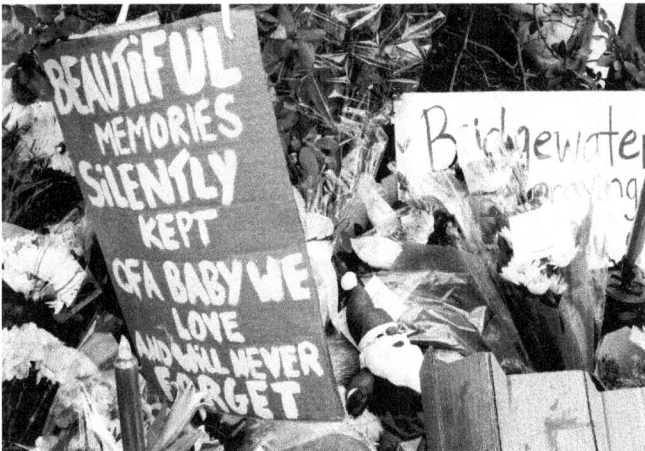

Another message, surrounded by bunches of flowers and candles, was written in white paint on a large piece of cardboard: *"Beautiful memo-*

ries silently kept of a baby we love and will never forget".

Other messages from family and friends were interspersed with messages from families in the local community. All the names of slain children were written on a soccer ball: *"Caroline, Jessica, Noah, Charlotte ..."* and children's books and toys were placed along with messages: *"Beautiful Angels Rest in Peace".*

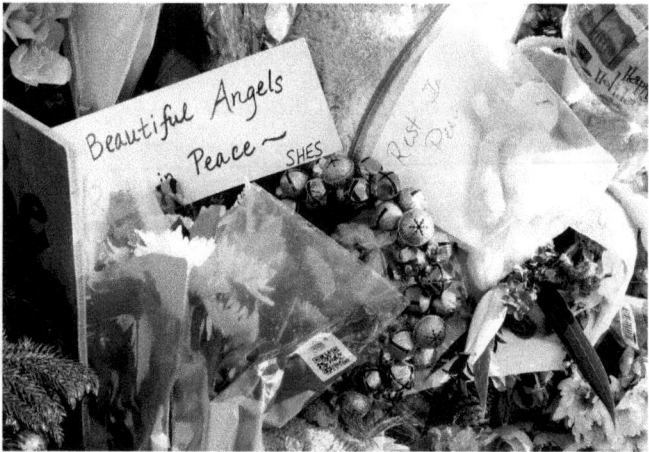

Some of the messages were of support for the community: *"Newtown and the world will remember each and every one of you forever."* Letters written personally to the families of the children who had been shot were tucked in between the flowers. One letter entitled *"What I Know"* was from a mother who had also lost her child: *"I am so sorry for your loss from somewhere so deep all I can feel is sorrow for what you and your loved ones must endure. It has been four long years since I lost my dear child, a ray of sunshine, a gift from God. Over those four years I have learned so many things I need to share with all of you who have a loss so great it cannot be put into words…"*

Being there and then afterward analyzing the photos it seemed as if the people who came with gifts were trying to create a communal space – both physical and psychological – in which they could imagine the dead children continuing to live.

People disassociate themselves from the horror of the unimaginable and, rendered helpless, and en masse they withdrew from the inhumane reality of the massacre. "I'll teach you how to jump on the wind's back, and then away we go," Peter says, the everlasting child, in J.M. Barrie's Peter Pan.

It is as if the people who wrote messages and brought toys could hear Peter saying, "All the world is made of faith, and trust, and pixie dust," to Tinker Bell, who has also been placed amongst the flowers.

Woody, an old family toy from Toy Story, is also present. "Reach for the sky!" Woody shouts. "I'd like to join your posses boys, but first I'm gonna sing a little song". And Buzz Light Year the Space-man says, "Don't worry, Woody. In just a few hours you'll be sitting around a campfire with Andy making delicious hot Schmoes."

Curious George was there too. Ted, the man with the yellow hat says, "Anyone can memorize facts and figures, the key is to just venture into the unknown and let your curiosity take hold". Win-nie-the-Pooh Bears and Tiggers were also there, and SpongeBob and Patrick, the starfish, Spider-Man, Minnie Mouse, and Hello Kitty.

It was in this way that people stricken by grief found ways to be empathic and keep hope alive, even though so many children had died. They ex-perienced "sensory fragmentation," but they also managed to find ways to integrate traumatic ex-periences and other imaginings, recombining metaphors to transform meaning and hold on to the dead children.

"I think we dream so we don't have to be apart for so long," Pooh said. "If we're in each other's dreams, we can be together all the time."

Together through metaphor the people cre-ated an alternate reality, an expression of the fullness of humanity, *consciously* gathering together, in vigils of love and solidarity.

We are Sandy Hook. We choose love.

We are together. We are family. We are hope. We are love.

Together we are strong.

God Bless 20 Precious Little Souls and 6 Amazing Brave Souls.

Rest in Peace Little Ones

We won't forget you Sandy Hook Elementary School (hand prints of small children)

"So the real importance of being conscious," Elio Frattaroli write, in *Healing the Soul in the Age of the Brain,* is that it allows us to become better people. It opens us to love and a genuine sense of community with our fellow human beings. It inspires us to live in accord with our high values, and to recognize and change the patterns of suffering we inflict (on ourselves as well as others) through unreflective enactment of our repetition compulsions."

On that cold December day in Newtown when

people came and left messages of condolence and placed teddy bears and flowers there was a genuine sense of community. Pastors, ministers, rabbis, grief counselors, service dogs, were ready to offer comfort and support. There was even a woman with "FREE HUGS" written and a poster with the message, "Let there be peace on Earth and let it begin with me".

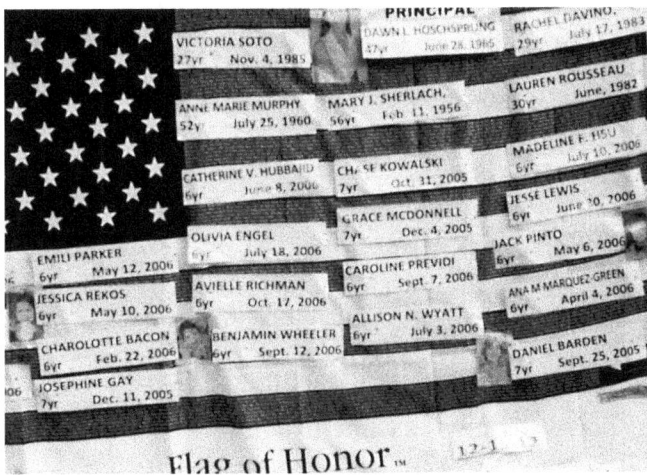

Other signs included the American flag. The names of the 20 kindergarten children, their principal, school psychologist, and teachers, with their ages and date of birth were written on pieces of paper and pinned to the flag. Woven into the fabric beneath the Stars and Stripes were the words "Flag of Honor", inspiring us to live in accord with our high values, and to recognize and change the patterns of suffering we inflict on ourselves as well as others. It is the noble ideal of the United States of America.

There were quotes from Shakespeare and messages reminiscent of Churchill and a dead King: "When all is lost, even in our darkest hour, hope will prevail". But it was Lincoln and his eulogy to a dead president that was in the ether of the moment. Almost palpable, was the stricken by grief desire for kindergarten children and the educators who tried to protect them to have not died in vain. And so it was that the living dedicated themselves that day, with some people actually writing in their cards their resolve to be a "better person". Together they imagined life as it could be otherwise. It was a rebirth of sorts, perhaps closer to the original intent of Lincoln's Gettysburg Address and undoubtedly more heartfelt than any modern day politician's resolve that "government of the people, by the people, for the people, shall not perish from the earth".

There was one sign that said, "Stay Strong, "LOVE >HATE", but on that day there were no messages of anger or hate. And yet there was one message that stood out: "We have everything, we have nothing, small and unstable we self destruct. We are sleeping sheep and there are wolves among us". It was written on the stone under the bridge in black spray paint although it looked as if it had been first written in white paint. Someone must have stood in the water to write it.

On one sign there were three lines from the 9-11 poem, "May your smiles bring us strength/ May your dreams bring us hope/May your innocence bring us faith". Emily Dickinson's "Unable are the loved to die/ For love is immortality" was placed amongst the flowers in a frame; and Helen Keller's "What we once enjoyed and deeply loved we can never lose/ For all that we love deeply be-

comes a part of us" was also there. Similarly, Mary
Elizabeth Frye's beloved poem:

> Do not stand at my grave and weep,
> I am not there; I do not sleep.
> I am a thousand winds that blow,
> I am the diamond glints on snow,
> I am the sun on ripened grain,
> I am the gentle autumn rain.
> When you awaken in the morning's hush
> I am the swift uplifting rush
> Of quiet birds in circling flight.
> I am the soft starlight at night.
> Do not stand at my grave and cry,
> I am not there; I did not die.

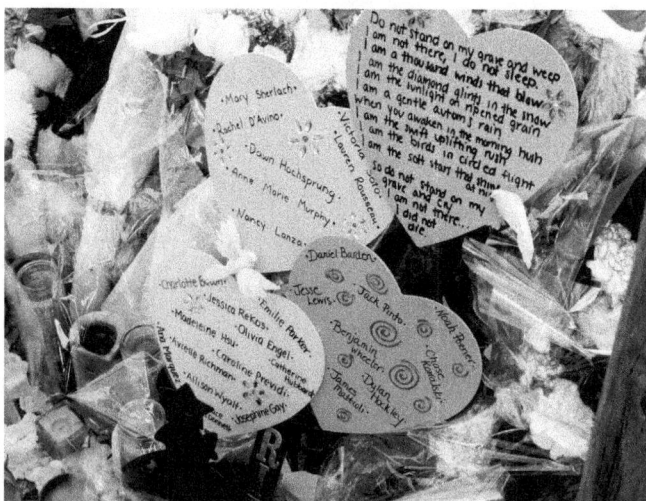

In Newtown it was possible to "see" people reach inside themselves and imagine life as it could be otherwise, and to reach out to those around them who had suffered a great loss. People stood in quiet contemplation, some praying, and as they moved along they searched amongst the flowers for messages tucked away, making sure every prayer and poem was read, and that every toy with writing on it, including a teddy bear's ears and feet with the children's names upon them, was not passed by unread. Somehow in that moment, the metaphors created by this word work connected mourners in ways that would not have been possible otherwise. Strangers hugged, held on to each other, or just stood in the middle of the crowd and cried, comforted by words they read, including the lines from a song by Eric Clapton, who has also lost a child, "Tears of heaven/ Beyond the door there's peace I'm sure."

"All decent people feel sorrow and righteous fury about the latest slaughter of innocents," the *New York Times* stated on December 4, 2015, following a massacre in San Bernardino, California. It was the first editorial on the front page of the newspaper in 95 years.

"It is a moral outrage and a national disgrace that people can legally purchase weapons designed specifically to kill with brutal speed and efficiency," the Editorial Board stated. "These are weapons of war, barely modified and deliberately marketed as tools of macho vigilantism and even insurrection." The Editorial Board leaves no doubt. "Let's be clear," they write. "These spree killings are all, in their own ways, acts of terrorism."

BOB DYLAN WRITES, "YES, 'N' HOW MANY DEATHS WILL IT TAKE TILL HE KNOWS THAT TOO MANY PEOPLE HAVE DIED?"

Everyday, politicians and the media create divisions and play on people's worst fears about the widely accepted phenomenon of the radicalization of youth by foreign terrorist groups, but there is almost virtually *no discussion* of the radicalization of youth in America into U.S. gun culture, or the radicalization of the U.S. Congress.

There were 1,516,863 gun deaths between 1968 and 2015 in the U.S., which is more than than entire cumulative war deaths (1,396,733) since the American Revolution[2]. Add to this sta-

---

2   "More Americans have died from guns in the

tistic that the Institute for Economics and Peace reports that the economic impact of violence was $13.6 trillion in 2015 or 13.3% of world GDP. Clearly not all gun deaths were caused by the use of military style automatic weapons and the global economic cost of violence is not solely due to the sale and use of automatic weapons in the U.S., but separating these deaths and the vast profits from armament sales cannot be done rationally or scientifically.

The pro-gun Senators who voted against the 2013 Assault Weapons Ban bill treated the killing of 20 young children and six adults in the Sandy Hook Massacre as if they were nothing more than collateral damage – the unintended consequences of friendly fire of man's most lucrative industry. Since the Sandy Hook Massacre (to date, July 4th, 2016) there have been another 1,002 mass shootings in the U.S. -- including massacres at the Emanuel African Methodist Episcopal Church in Charleston, SC (June 17, 2015) and at the Pulse Nightclub in Orlando (June 12, 2016)– and at

---

United States since 1968 than on battlefields of all the wars in American history." Nicholas Kristof wrote on Thursday, August 26th, 2015 in his column in the New York Times.

least 1,135 people have been killed and 3,953 have been wounded. In 2014 alone there were 51,818 gun incidents, 12,588 deaths, and 277 mass shootings; in 2015 there were 53,287 gun incidents, 13,432 deaths, and 331 mass shootings; and by mid-June 2016 there have already been 24,632 gun incidents, 6,333 deaths, and, including Dallas, 146 mass shootings.

At the time of the 2013 Assault Weapons Ban bill one of the pro-gun Senators spoke on Fox and at the Hoover Institute about the "principled men in office (who) keep the U.S. from tyranny" and in that context he talked of "the power and transmission of ideas". The idea of "principled men in office et cetera" is an ideological stance that is constantly re-established through "the transmission of ideas" promulgated through banal hypothetical arguments falsely presented as "truth". It is the reason the Assault Weapons Ban bill was so easy kill.

In other words, the arguments *against* the bill were ideological and *theoretical,* while the arguments *for* the bill were based on heinous *real events* and tragic human experience. Thus is was possible for   ideological and hypothetical "despair" of a pro-gun testifier to be effectively used to counter and co-opt the very real grief of a father whose son had been killed and the trauma doctor on duty in the ER when the mass shooting occurred. The following quote presents the rationale:

> It is not the task of a theoretician to determine the varying degrees in which a cause can be realized, but to establish the cause as such: that is to say: he must concern himself less with the road than with the goal. In this, however, the basic correctness of an idea is decisive and not the difficulty of its execution. As soon as the theoretician attempts to take account of so-called 'utility' and 'reality' instead of the absolute truth, his work will cease to be a polar star of seeking humanity and instead will become a prescription for everyday life.

This quote is from *Mein Kampf,* and so is the quote that follows:

> The theoretician of a movement must lay down its goal, the politician strive for

its fulfillment. The thinking of the one, therefore, will be determined by eternal truth, the actions of the other more by the practical reality of the moment. The greatness of the one lies in the absolute abstract soundness of his idea, that of the other in his correct attitude toward the given facts and their advantageous application; and in this the theoretician's aim must serve as his guiding star.

Many people have died through the ages because of the hypotheticals of theoreticians. Human fallibility and errors of judgment are ignored for delusionary "truths". Pathologies reside in the individual but also in societies. Group psychosis can be rationalized, legitimized, normalized. Words can be twisted into narrative loops so that the pro-gun Senators in the U.S. Congress can come up with arguments that it is moral and decent to protect the gun and kill the child. How long will it be till they wake up to the eternal truth that too many children have died?

At the February 27, 2013 news conference held by Senator Dianne Feinstein announcing the presentation of the Assault Weapons Ban bill to the U.S. Congress, many people spoke and addressed this question.

"As people of faith we have the moral obligation to stand with and for the victims of gun violence and end it," the Reverend Gary Hall said. "Everyone in this city seems to live in terror of the gun lobby. Together we have tolerated school shootings and mall shootings and theater shootings and workplace shooting, and temple and church shootings and neighborhood shootings for far too long. Enough is enough. Together we must stand together as people of all faiths across the religious landscape of America."

"Weapons designed for the military to kill large numbers of people in combat are replicated for civilian use," Senator Feinstein said. "They fall into the hands, one way or the other, of grievance killers, of gangs, of those who are mentally unstable or ill. They are sold out of the trunks and back seats of automobiles in cities, as well as gun shows, with no question asked. Massacres have taken place in businesses, law practices, malls, movie theaters, and especially schools. These massacres don't seem to stop . . . And the common thread in these shootings is that each gunman used a semiautomatic assault weapon or large capacity ammunition magazine."

"I'm going to talk from my heart," Senator Carolyn McCarthy said. "I've met so many victims over the years, and in Congress nobody wanted to touch the issue and in the last several years the massacres were going on more and more and I kept saying what's wrong with all of us? How many people have to be killed before we do something? . . . You know, we have been meeting with the NRA over the last few weeks to try to find how we could work together. It's been frustrating. I still have great hope, but to be honest with you I am not going to be able to trust them to be there for the tough votes."

Senator McCarthy talked of "NRA members speaking out to get something done." She said, "These are law abiding citizens. They want to hunt. They want to go duck hunting. And yet, we have these machines. We have the large magazines that can take down twenty children in seconds, and the only reason that the slaughter stopped is because our first responders were there and the killer ended up taking his own life. It has to stop. It has to stop. We can make a difference and we can save thousands and thousands of lives."

"We will do the right thing," Senator McCarthy continued. "Our police officers will do the right thing. But if the American people don't stand up to the lies that are being said, that we can't do anything about gun violence, who loses? Our children. They are the ones who lose. We can do this. Be out there for us. Thank you."

"This isn't a matter of the Constitution," Senator Dick Durbin said. "It's an issue of conscience. We have one basic question, which is being asked today, which I hope we can answer: What does it take? What does it take to move a nation? What does it take to move a Congress? . . . What does it take? It took twenty children in Newtown Connecticut and six adults of extraordinary courage to risk their lives to try and save and protect those children. It was the image of those children that each and everyone of us looked at and said that could be my son or my daughter, that could be my grandson, that could be my granddaughter. And it made a difference. It was the tipping point in this national conversation . . .. The question is: what will we do about it? We can only do as much as the American people help us do. We need their support. Their silence can't win the issue. They have to speak out. . . . We need them to step up. We need their voices as part of this conversation.

Senator Richard Blumenthal spoke next. "This is a historic occasion," he said. "A signature moment in this profoundly significant effort to achieve and end gun violence in our country. . . "I would particularly like to thank the law enforcement community who are here today. . . I have listened to our police, our prosecutors, our law enforcement community, . . . I have listened to them in countless forums and numerous tragedies and they have said to me, 'Do something about the guns. Ban the assault weapons and prohibit the high capacity magazines.' And a number of the police who came to Newton said to me, 'we could not have stopped the shooter. Even with body armor, with the body armor we were wearing with that kind of assault weapon shooting at us.'

"Our law enforcement community is outgunned by criminals and mentally ill people, and domestic abusers who have assault weapons and should be separated from those weapons. I am listening to them but I am also listening to the people of Newtown. Senator Durbin is right. I was there the afternoon parents arrived at the Sandy Hook firehouse." Senator Blumenthal stopped. He continued his voice trembling and close to tears. "I came there as a public official but what I saw was through the eyes of a parent and I will never forget the sights and sounds of that day as parents emerged from that firehouse learning that their five and six year old children would not be coming home that night."

" I am listening to the people of Newtown and Connecticut who have said to me, 'we have to do something about the guns' and we need to keep faith with them . . . My hope is we will seize this moment with a sense of urgency and passion and sustain this momentum over the hard fight, make no mistake it will be a hard fight ahead, and always, always, remember Newtown and keep faith with its victims."

Senator Christopher Murphy followed. "Dick and I and Elizabeth were there that day and as a father of a four year old and a one year old there are a lot of moments when I wish I could take back what I saw – that heaving incomprehensible grief that comes especially in those first moments of trying to understand what just happened."

"Let me tell you what's happening today in Newtown Connecticut." Senator Murphy continued. "Sandy Hook Elementary School has moved and a lot of teachers haven't come back and a lot of students haven't returned. But in each one of these classrooms there's a safe word. In one third grade classroom it's 'monkey' and a couple of time every day a kid yells out that safe word when he gets into a conversation with a fellow student that he doesn't want to be part of – a third grader talking about what he saw that day, the bodies he stepped over, the look that he caught in the shooter's eye. That's what happening in Newtown. That's what's happens in one of these communicates that deals with these mass atrocities. It's not just the families that grieve. It the trauma that washes over whole communities, like waves, in the weeks and months afterwards. Kids would be alive today in Newtown, Connecticut if the law we are proposing today were in place on December 14th 2012. It's as simple as that. Why do we know that? We know that because the data tells us that. Despite what the gun lobby will say."

"Forty percent of the mass killings in this country -- *in the history* of this country --have happened since the assault weapon ban expired," Senator Murphy said. "More kids would be alive today in Newtown today, because we know what the numbers tell us. We also know what happened that day. We know that most of these incidents end when the shooter has to reload, either the gun jams or people intervene. You know what -- to get off one hundred rounds that day in about a ten minute period of time Adam Lanza had to reload twice."

"We know that if this law was in place on December 14th there would be little girls and boys alive today," Senator Murphy said. "The gun lobby has said over and over again in the last several weeks that this is just a feel good piece of legislation. You know, they are right about that. It would feel really good if Alison and Charlotte and Daniel and Olivier and Josephine and Anna had got to enjoy Christmas with their parents. It would feel really good if Dylan and Madeline and Kathryn and Chase and Jesse and James took the bus to school this morning. It would feel really good if Grace and Emily and Jack and Noah and Carolyn and Jessica and Ariel and Ben were alive today. It would feel really good if parents all across this country didn't have to wake up every morning worrying that without action their kids are at risk just like those kids in Newtown. This is going to be hard. This is going to be difficult. But to honor those twenty lives and six more in Newtown we're going to get it done."

After many people had spoken Michael Nutter, the Mayor of Philadelphia, stood up. "Again, again, and again," he began, "Americans have been stunned by senseless violence in acts involving assault weapons and large capacity magazines." Mayor Nutter names the massacres until he reaches Sandy Hook. "And on December 14, 2012, tragedy struck again, killing twenty children and 6 educators in Newtown, Connecticut in an act that still remains incomprehensible to all of us. Too many times in the last years mayors have expressed shock at mass shootings. Even more frequently many of us must cope with gun violence that occurs on the streets of our cities day after day after day. Weapons of mass destruction are destroying our communities, our streets, and our families." He speaks of the police officer killed with an AK 47 and the impact on his family. "Tell any mother or father or sister or brother or niece of nephew why their family member is no longer with us because of these finds of weapons and handguns with high capacity magazines. Why does anyone need on those?" He points to the automatic weapons on a screen.

"This death and destruction must end right now," Mayor Nutter said. "This must stop. The legislation that Senator Feinstein and others are introducing today will help to end the insanity. I am here to register today the strong support of the U.S. Conference of Mayors for the Assault Weapons Ban of 2013 and we commit as an organization, hundreds of mayors all across America, small, medial and large cities. We are committed to doing everything necessary to ensure that this legislation becomes law."

"I have for you today a letter originally sent just 3 days after the Newtown tragedy occurred and now signed by 210 mayors across the country which calls on the President and the Congress to take immediate action to make reasonable changes in our gun laws and regulations. Listed first in that letter was our recommendation for the enactment of legislation to ban assault weapons and high capacity magazines that has now been presented by Senator Diane Feinstein and others in this bill. "

The last word goes to Charles Ramsey, the Police Commissioner of Philadelphia. "Today I am speaking on behalf of the major Police Chief's Association, made up of the 63 largest cities in the United States and I have the honor of serving as President of that organization," Commissioner Ramsey stated. He spoke also of the International Association of Chiefs of Police, which he stated, "is the largest of all the police organizations and they want me to pass on to you their full support for the legislation."

"But I am also here to speak for myself," he said. "I've been in law enforcement more than forty years as Police Chief in Washington D.C. and for the last 5 years I've been Police Commissioner in Philadelphia. I've seen a lot of violence over that period of time but nothing compares with the devastation caused by assault weapons . . . I don't think that people really understand the firepower that's out there on the streets that our officers have to face everyday and the citizens in our cities have to face everyday. To my left is a display of weapons. I don't claim to be an expert in the workings of a firearm, but I am an expert in terms of understanding the carnage that they cause on the streets of our cities."

Commissioner Ramsey points at four of the weapons and names the massacres in which each weapon was used including "the Bushmaster XM 15, a military style assault weapon that was used in the Newtown massacre – that's exactly what it was ..."

"Twenty children slaughtered at one time in a school house in a town that many of us in this room probably never heard of until this happened. A town that you just wouldn't expect something like this to take place. If the slaughter of twenty babies does not capture and hold your attention then I give up," the Commissioner shakes his head, "because I don't know what will."

"We have to pass legislation. We can't allow the legislation to get so watered down and filled with loop holes that it is meaningless and won't do anything." He points at the military style weapons. "How are you going to go hunting with something like that? If you kill something there's nothing left to eat." For the first time there is laughter.

The Commissioner ends by stating, "We are not trying to seize everybody's guns but we need reasonable gun control in this country or guess what it will happen again."

A PARTING SHOT: THEORY VERSUS LIVED EXPERIENCE

The 2013 Assault Weapons Ban bill failed and more mass killings have occurred, including the San Bernardino Massacre, the Charleston Church Massacre, the Orlando Massacre, and the Dallas Massacre – and each time there is a mass killing the outrage of the public grows stronger but the gun lobby does not grow weaker.

Following the Orlando Massacre a 15-hour filibuster by Senator Christopher Murphy of Connecticut, and a 26-hour sit-in on the floor of the U.S. House of Representatives did not shift the pro-gun Senate or House and the bills on universal background checks and a ban on gun purchases by those on federal watch lists failed.

There is now a general consensus that there will be no gun legislation passed in 2016. But the American public must not give up. Democracy cannot be so reduced and undermined. We must honor the memory of our loved ones and right the wrongs to the American people condoned by the U.S. Congress under a veneer of legitimacy and re-spectability, and by Senators and Member of the House of Representatives who built the theoretical arguments to protect automatic weapons that defeated the 2013 Assault Weapons Ban bill and blocked the 2016 bills.

An analysis of the public record of the Hearings and subcommittee meetings of the 2013 Assault Weapons Ban bill reveals: *mass deception and that the public is being misled.*

Disassociate the gun from violence. Feminize it. Avoid attending the hearings when descriptions are given of what happened to the children. Don't listen. Co-opt the grief. Grieve for the gun. Tell stories of how you got your gun. Associate it with valor. Attach it to theories that must be protected. Make these theories more important than American lives. More important than a million of them. More important than the dead children.

Don't talk about the children. Steer clear of the images of them dying. Being blown away. Eleven bullets in a tiny body. Obliterate the image. Do it and appear caring and thoughtful. Be theoreticians.

Remember as it states in *Mein Kampf,* the theoretician of a movement must lay down his goal. Be the theoretician and the politician. The politician must strive for its fulfillment. The thinking of the one, therefore, will be determined by eternal truth, the actions of the other more by the practical reality of the moment. The greatness of the one lies in the absolute abstract soundness of his idea, that of the other in his correct attitude toward the given facts and their advantageous application, and in this the theoretician's aim must serve as his guiding star.

Millions of people have died because of these kinds of arguments that turn governments against the people. To ensure that America does not become a right-wing dictatorship cleverly concealed in democratic rhetoric that hides the madness of these most logically devised ideas, we must continually ask, "what about the children?" The theories we live by must protect them. Let the memory of the children who died in the massacre at Sandy

Hook be our guiding star. And for those who died in Charleston, San Bernardino, Orlando, Dallas and other shooting, the same question must be asked. For if the 2013 Assault Weapons Ban bill had passed those massacres might not have happened and certainly would not have happened in the same way. If we as a people are to regain our humanity keep asking: *What about the children?* Until the madness stops.

The members of the U.S. Congress who voted against the 2013 Assault Weapons Ban bill and the bills of 2016 must look at themselves and change their behavior. They can no longer represent the gun lobby that is selling military style guns such as the gun that killed the five and six year old children at Sandy Hook Elementary School. They need to know that democracy breaks down when those who govern condone violence that devours the nation's children. The U.S. Congress can no longer be blinded to the consequences of their actions. They must listen to the American people and the organizations that represent them. Here are the organizations that supported the 2013 Assault Weapons Ban bill to many of the official letters of support.

LAW ENFORCEMENT

Law enforcement organizations that supported the 2013 Assault Weapons Ban bill:

- International Association of Campus Law Enforcement Administrators
- International Association of Chiefs of Police
- Major Cities Chiefs Association
- National Association of Women Law Enforcement Executives
- National Law Enforcement Partnership to Prevent Gun Violence
- National Organization of Black Law Enforcement Executives
- Police Executive Research Forum
- Police Foundation
- Women in Federal Law Enforcement
- Chaska, Minn., Police Chief Scott Knight, former chairman of the Firearms Commit-

tee, International Association of Chiefs of Police

- Los Angeles County Sheriff Lee Baca
- Los Angeles Police Chief Charlie Beck
- San Diego Police Chief Bill Lansdowne

HEALTH CARE

Health care organizations that supported the 2013 Assault Weapons Ban bill.

- American Academy of Nursing
- American Academy of Pediatrics
- American College of Surgeons
- American Congress of Obstetricians and Gynecologists
- American Medical Association
- American Public Health Association
- Association for Ambulatory Behavioral Healthcare
- Doctors for America
- National Association of School Nurses
- National Physicians Alliance
- Physicians for Social Responsibility
- San Francisco Mental Health Association
- Society for the Advancement of Violence

and Injury Research

- Society of General Internal Medicine

EDUCATION AND CHILD WELFARE

Education and child welfare organizations that supported the 2013 Assault Weapons Ban bill.

- 20 Children
- American Federation of Teachers
- California Teachers Association
- Child Welfare League of America
- Children's Defense Fund
- Every Child Matters
- Los Angeles Community College District
- MomsRising
- National Association of Social Workers
- National PTA
- National Education Association
- New Schools Venture Fund
- San Diego Unified School District

- Save the Children
- United States Student Association

GUN SAFETY

Gun safety organizations that supported the 2013 Assault Weapons Ban bill.

- Arizonans for Gun Safety
- Brady Campaign to Prevent Gun Violence
- Ceasefire Oregon
- Coalition to Stop Gun Violence
- Hoosiers Concerned About Gun Violence
- Illinois Council Against Handgun Violence
- Law Center to Prevent Gun Violence
- Mayors Against Illegal Guns
- Ohio Coalition Against Gun Violence
- One Million Moms for Gun Control
- Protect Minnesota
- Stopourshootings.org
- Violence Policy Center
- Washington CeaseFire
- Wisconsin Anti-Violence Effort

- Women Against Gun Violence

RELIGIOUS

Religious organizations that supported the 2013 Assault Weapons Ban bill.

- African Methodist Episcopal Church
- Alliance of Baptists
- American Baptist Churches of the South
- American Baptist Home Mission Societies
- American Friends Service Committee
- Baptist Peace Fellowship of North America
- Camp Brotherhood
- Catholic Charities USA
- Catholic Health Association
- Catholic Health Initiatives
- Catholics in Alliance for the Common Good
- Catholics United
- Church of the Brethren
- Church Women United, Inc.
- Conference of Major Superiors of Men

- Disciples Home Missions, Christian Church (Disciples of Christ)
- Dominican Sisters of Peace
- Faiths United To Prevent Gun Violence
- Franciscan Action Network
- Friends Committee on National Legislation
- Health Ministries Association
- Heeding God's Call
- Hindu American Foundation
- Interfaith Alliance of Idaho
- Islamic Society of North America
- Jewish Council for Public Affairs
- Jewish Reconstructionist Movement
- Leadership Conference of Women Religious
- Mennonite Central Committee, Washington Office
- National Advocacy Center of the Sisters of the Good Shepherd
- National Council of Churches
- National Episcopal Health Ministries

- NETWORK, A National Catholic Social Justice Lobby
- Pathways Faith Community
- Pax Christi USA
- PICO Network Lifelines to Healing
- Presbyterian Church (U.S.A.) Office of Public Witness
- Progressive National Baptist Convention
- Rabbinical Assembly
- Religious Action Center of Reform Judaism
- San Francisco Interfaith Council
- Sikh Council on Religion and Education, USA
- Sisters of Mercy of the Americas
- Sojourners
- Unitarian Universalist Association of Congregations
- United Church of Christ
- United Methodist Church
- United Methodist Women
- United States Conference of Catholic Bishops Committee on Domestic Justice and

Human Development

- United Synagogue of Conservative Judaism
- Washington National Cathedral
- Women of Reform Judaism

OTHER ORGANIZATIONS

Other organizations that supported the 2013 Assault Weapons Ban bill.

- Alliance for Business Leadership
- American Bar Association
- Black American Political Association of California
- Center for American Progress Action Fund
- Grandmothers for Peace International
- League of Women Voters of the United States
- Los Angeles Gay & Lesbian Center
- NAACP
- National Parks Conservation Association
- Precision Remotes
- Sierra Club
- TASH
- VoteVets.org

- Washington Office on Latin America

LOCALITIES

Localities that supported the 2013 Assault Weapons Ban bill.

- U.S. Conference of Mayors
- National League of Cities
- Los Angeles County Board of Supervisors
- San Francisco Board of Supervisors
- San Luis Obispo County Supervisor Bruce Gibson
- Santa Cruz Board of Supervisors
- Ventura County Board of Supervisors
- Oakland Unified School District Superintendent Anthony Smith
- Boston City Council

FORMER GOVERNORS

Former governors who supported the 2013 Assault Weapons Ban bill.

- Former California Governor George Deukmejian
- Former Secretary of Homeland Secretary Tom Ridge

CURRENT SENATE COSPONSORS

Current Senate cosponsors who supported the 2013 Assault Weapons Ban bill.

- Senator Richard Blumenthal (D-Conn.)
- Senator Barbara Boxer (D-Calif.)
- Senator Ben Cardin (D-Md.)
- Senator Tom Carper (D-Del.)
- Senator Mo Cowan (D-Mass.)
- Senator Dick Durbin (D-Ill.)
- Senator Al Franken (D-Minn.)
- Senator Kirsten Gillibrand (D-N.Y.)
- Senator Tom Harkin (D-Iowa)
- Senator Mazie Hirono (D-Hawaii)
- Senator Amy Klobuchar (D-Minn.)
- Senator Frank Lautenberg (D-N.J.)
- Senator Carl Levin (D-Mich.)
- Senator Robert Menendez (D-N.J.)
- Senator Barbara Mikulski (D-Md.)

- Senator Chris Murphy (D-Conn.)

- Senator Patty Murray (D-Wash.)

- Senator Jack Reed (D-R.I.)

- Senator John Rockefeller (D-W.Va.)

- Senator Brian Schatz (D-Hawaii)

- Senator Charles Schumer (D-N.Y.)

- Senator Elizabeth Warren (D-Mass.)

- Senator Sheldon Whitehouse (D-R.I.)

MAYORS

Mayors who supported the 2013 Assault Weapons Ban bill.

- The group Mayors Against Illegal Guns in early February sent a letter to House and Senate leaders calling for support of the Assault Weapons Ban bill of 2013. The letter was signed by 886 mayors from cities across the country.

- The mayors of San Francisco, Los Angeles, Sacramento, San Jose, Long Beach, Oakland, San Diego and Santa Ana wrote a letter supporting the bill in January.

CALIFORNIA CITIES

California cities that supported the 2013 Assault Weapons Ban bill.

- Beverly Hills;
- Calabasas;
- Del Mar;
- Encinitas;
- Lemon Grove;
- Los Angeles;
- National City;
- Petaluma;
- San Francisco;
- Santa Rosa;
- Stockton;
- Ventura;
- West Hollywood

ABOUT DENNY TAYLOR

Denny Taylor is a lifelong activist and scholar committed to nurturing the imagination and human spirit. She regards art, literature, and science inseparable. She has organized more than 30 international scholars' forums, and speaks to diverse national and international audiences on a broad range of issues.

In 1983, Taylor published Family Literacy, which is regarded a classic in the field; Growing Up Literate received the MLA Shaughnessy award in 1988; and Toxic Literacies, published in 1996, was nominated for both the Pulitzer Prize and the National Book Award. In 2004, Taylor was inducted into the IRA's Reading Hall of Fame. She is Professor Emeritus of Literacy Studies at Hofstra University, and the founder and CEO of Garn Press. Her most recent books are Save Our Children, Save Our School, Pearson Broke the Golden Rule, Rosie's Umbrella, Rat-a-tat-tat! I've Lost My Cat! which received the Gelett Burgess Children's Book Award, and Split Second Solution.

BOOKS BY DENNY TAYLOR

Split Second Solution: Denny Taylor. Garn Press, August 2016.

Great Women Scholars: Yetta Goodman, Maxine Greene, Louise Rosenblatt, Margaret Meek Spencer: Garn Press, March 2016.

Rat-a-tat-tat! I've Lost My Cat!: Garn Press, November 2015.

The Romance of Mathematics: Garn Press, June 2015.

Rosie's Umbrella: Garn Press, January 2015.

Save Our Children, Save Our School, Pearson Broke the Golden Rule: Garn Press, July 2014.

Nineteen Clues: Great Transformations Can Be Achieved Through Collective Action: Garn Press, June 2014.

Beginning to Read and the Spin Doctors of Science: The Political Campaign to Change America's Mind About How Children Learn to Read: National Council of Teachers of English (NCTE), June 1998.

Many Families, Many Literacies: An International Declaration of Principles: Heinemann. May 1997.

Teaching and Advocacy: (with Debbie Coughlin and Joanna Marasco). Stenhouse, January 1997.

Toxic Literacies: Exposing the Injustice of Bureaucratic Texts: Heinemann, September 1996.

From The Child's Point Of View: Heinemann, September 1993.

Learning Denied: Heinemann, November 1990.

Growing Up Literate, Learning From Inner City Families: (with Catherine Dorsey-Gaines). Heinemann, June 1988.

Family Storybook Reading: (with Dorothy S. Strickland). Heinemann, July 1986.

Family Literacy: Young Children Learning to Read and Write: Heinemann, March 1983 (1st edition), December 1998 (2nd edition).

www.ingramcontent.com/pod-product-compliance
Lightning Source LLC
Chambersburg PA
CBHW071240020426
42333CB00015B/1552